Original title:
Flora and Fables

Copyright © 2025 Creative Arts Management OÜ
All rights reserved.

Author: Isaac Ravenscroft
ISBN HARDBACK: 978-1-80567-077-3
ISBN PAPERBACK: 978-1-80567-157-2

Chronicles Cast in Cow Parsley Light

In the glade where flowers dance,
A dandelion took a chance.
With a wig made from soft moss,
He claimed he was the boss!

Bees in tuxedos buzzed around,
Critiquing blooms they barely found.
One said, "You're looking spry,
But your pollen's running dry!"

A ladybug, all decked in red,
Said, "Stop the talk! Let's find some bread!"
So off they rolled, in search of snacks,
While laughing at their flowery hacks.

In sunlight's gentle, twinkling glow,
A cat ran by, with quite the show.
He thought he was a blooming beast,
But tripped and nosed an artichoke feast!

A Symphony of Leaves

In a park where trees do sway,
The squirrels play their wild ballet.
The leaves all whisper, 'Let's have fun!'
As acorns roll beneath the sun.

A trumpet flower shouts, 'Take heed!'
While others laugh at dandelion seed.
The sunbeams tickle every bough,
And laughter bursts from trees somehow.

The Oak's Ancient Wisdom

An oak sat wise, with bark like cheer,
It told young buds, 'Just lend an ear.'
'In life, don't fret about the score,
Unless it's birds singing—then ask for more!'

Branches stretched in playful jest,
While creatures passed, they felt so blessed.
'Twist and twirl, don't stand so still,
For every quirk, there's time to fill!'

Tales of the Hidden Grove

In hidden nooks, the critters meet,
Where mushrooms dance on tiny feet.
A hedgehog spins a yarn so bright,
Telling tales of the moonlit night.

With giggles soft from shadows dear,
A rabbit hops, "Have you heard here?"
A hedgerow's gossip fills the air,
In this green world, they have no care.

A Dance of Daisies

A daisy chain forms on the ground,
As bees buzz 'round without a sound.
The petals sway in giggles bright,
A flower party, pure delight!

With butterflies as guests, so nice,
They waltz around, oh-so precise.
Fluffs of pollen do a jig,
In the sun, they spin and swig!

Adventures in the Aromatic Abyss

In a garden where scents collide,
A spritz of thyme took a wild ride.
Rosemary laughed in a herbal spree,
As garlic danced, setting the bees free.

Chives rolled around, in quite a whirl,
While basil did cartwheels, showing its twirl.
A minty breeze caused a ruckus galore,
With petunias gossiping about the decor.

Glory of the Glistening Geranium

Oh, the geranium pranced in the sun,
With petals so bright, it thought it was fun.
It waved to the daisies, 'Come join my quirk!'
While pansies giggled, yelling, 'Let's lurk!'

A bumblebee buzzed with a silly chuckle,
As lilies insisted on forming a huddle.
A big bloom blurted, 'Let's have a ball!'
The garden was buzzing, all creatures enthralled.

Burgeoning Myths of the Blooming Cactus

The cactus dreamed it was a tall green tree,
Yet tripped on itself, oh dear, what a spree!
With spines like armor, it strutted around,
Challenging breeze, not making a sound.

In the desert it claimed the title of sage,
Telling tales of water, like unturned page.
But every slight breeze sent it reeling back,
'Oh, how I wish for an oceanic snack!'

The Treetop Tales Unfashioned

In the branches high up, the leaves would convene,
A squirrel in a suit said, 'I look quite serene!'
With acorns as jewels and bark as their dress,
They threw a grand party, causing a mess.

Frogs jumped on branches, mimicking tunes,
While owls hooted rhythms under the moons.
The laughter was loud; the ruckus was real,
In a top-tier retreat, that's how they would feel.

Whims of the Wisteria

A wisteria danced in a breeze,
With blossoms that tickled the trees.
It borrowed a hat,
From a cat that sat,
And went to a party with ease.

The other flowers stared in surprise,
As it twirled under bright, sunny skies.
"What a charming show!"
They all yelled, "Bravo!"
With laughter that lit up their eyes.

The Limerick of the Lush Landscape

In a meadow where daisies do prance,
A deer took the time to enhance.
He wore a green tie,
And said with a sigh,
"Grass is just grass, but I like to dance!"

The squirrels would giggle and cheer,
As the flowers would whisper, "Oh dear!"
"What a sight to see,
A deer full of glee,
He's the jester of all far and near!"

Pearl of the Poppy's Heart

A poppy once dreamed of a pearl,
And in her vast dreams she would twirl.
    She searched near and far,
    For a shiny bright star,
And found it amidst all the swirl.

She wore it with pride on her head,
Saying, "Look at my jewel, so red!"
    The bees buzzed in awe,
    Saying, "What a flaw!"
For a flower, it's quite out of thread.

The Story of the Gentle Grass

There once was some grass, oh so meek,
Who loved to play hide-and-seek.
It hid from the sun,
Just to have fun,
And giggled whenever they'd peek.

One day it was tickled by dew,
And laughed till the whole meadow grew.
The flowers joined in,
With a chuckle and spin,
Creating a joyful review.

Moonlit Meadows and Myths

In moonlit meadows, cows wear capes,
They leap like frogs, doing silly scrapes.
The owls hold council, with glasses askew,
While rabbits debate if the moon's really blue.

With fireflies winking like stars on a spree,
A hedgehog recites from a book of decree.
The mushrooms are giggling in morning's soft glow,
As snails tell tall tales of the friends they know.

The Dance of Dandelion Wishes

Dandelions twirl in the soft summer air,
Swaying and spinning without a care.
Each puff a wish on the breeze it will ride,
While ladybugs gossip, all plump and tied.

The bees throw a party, all buzzing with cheer,
While the ants carry crumbs, their own buffet near.
They laugh at the clovers adorned in their green,
Dancing together, a most merry scene.

Echoes of the Ancient Grove

In the ancient grove where squirrels tell tales,
The trees lean in close, sharing their gales.
A fox in a top hat gives lectures on cheese,
While raccoons critique, on bended knees.

The echo of laughter floats high in the leaves,
As bunnies sketch maps of the tricks up their sleeves.
Their shadows are frolicking, telling their truths,
In this realm of the whimsical, nature uncouth.

Serpents in the Sunflower Field

In sunlit fields where the sunflowers grin,
A serpent ties knots while trying to spin.
The daisies all chuckle, their petals a-flutter,
As the wind stirs the gossip, a lighthearted clutter.

A turtle, quite slow, joins the dance with a sigh,
While crickets compose a sweet melody sly.
The sunflowers wink with their faces of gold,
As the laughter of nature gracefully unfolds.

The Myth of the Mountain Fern

In a forest so dense, where no critters tread,
Lived a fern with claims that it could see ahead.
It wore tiny glasses, stitched from a snail's shell,
Pretending to know the secrets so well.

The treefolk would chuckle as they passed by,
For the fern had no notion it was a sly lie.
'Look at me,' said the fern, 'I can see the rain!'
But all it could glimpse was the old mossy grain.

One day a squirrel, with acorn in tow,
Challenged the fern, 'Tell me, where does wind blow?'
The fern scratched its fronds and began to hum,
With a voice like a broom, it could barely strum.

So next time you wander where the ferns might dwell,
Remember their tales, both true and a spell.
For in every green leaf, there's mischief and cheer,
In myths spun by plants, one's laughter draws near.

Whimsies Among the Wildflowers

A daisy once bragged it could dance in the air,
While tulips just giggled, 'You haven't a prayer!'
But the daisy kept twirling, its petals in flight,
Claiming it's surely the star of the night.

The rose tried to join with a pirouette,
But thorny mishaps were its only debt.
It pranced and it tripped on the turf with a crash,
While the daisies just squeaked, 'You're not part of our sash!'

Beneath a bright sun with glee in their heart,
The wildflowers plotted a most clever chart.
They'd challenge the daisies to a grand contest,
To see who could bloom in the silliest dress.

So if you wander where blossoms convene,
Keep an eye on their antics, oh what a scene!
For in every petal, there's laughter to find,
In whimsical worlds where the wildflowers bind.

The Chronicles of the Climbing Ivy

There once was a vine that dreamt it could be,
A great mountain climber, so fancy and free.
It crept up the walls with a gaze full of pride,
Saying, 'I'm scaling the heights; I won't be denied!'

But alas, it would slip on the bricks made of clay,
And tumble back down, what a shameful display!
The gardener watched with a grin on his face,
As the ivy sprawled out like a wide, green embrace.

One day a wise snail crawled by with a drawl,
'Why not take it easy, dear ivy, not fall?'
But the ivy just laughed and tried harder to climb,
Declaring, 'I can do it, just give me some time!'

So next time you see a vine trying to soar,
Remember the tale of the ivy's uproar.
For sometimes ambition can lead you astray,
In the most tangled stories, fun often plays.

Boughs of Secrets After Rain

When raindrops blanket the leaves with a sigh,
The branches confide to the clouds passing by.
They whisper of flowers, of gossip and glee,
Of how bees steal honey and sing out of key.

A birch once proclaimed, 'I'm the best for a chat,
I know all the rumors, like where squirrels are at.'
But the oaks would just chuckle, 'Dear birch, don't you see,
We're ancient and wise; let us spill all the tea!'

With a twinkle of dew, secrets twirl in the air,
As the trunks tell tall tales, without a single care.
A tale of a rabbit who fancied a hat,
Worn sideways in spring as it raced with a cat.

So listen to boughs when the rain softly falls,
For every great story in nature enthralls.
In a chorus of whispers from branches so low,
Funny fables unravel as breezes all blow.

The Twilight of the Tulip Tree

At dusk the tulip starts to grin,
With petals twitching, where to begin?
A squirrel jokes beneath its shade,
Spilling secrets the wind had made.

The branches dance, they wiggle and sway,
While bugs throw parties, hip-hip hooray!
One beetle boasts of his shiny shell,
While ladybugs laugh—oh, do tell, do tell!

Nearby, the daisies gossip in rows,
About a bumblebee who's lost his pose.
He buzzes loud but can't find the queen,
In the merriment of the big green scene.

The frogs croak rhymes, some silly, some wise,
The tulip chuckles and rolls its eyes.
All nature joins in this twilight's cheer,
With giggles and grins, it's the best time of year!

In the Arms of the Weeping Willow.

Beneath the willow, shadows sway,
The branches tell tales of a long lost day.
A raccoon sneaks with a mischievous twinkle,
While the crickets hum their nightly sprinkle.

A snail sets up his slow parade,
With tiny flags, a grand charade.
The willow chuckles, its leaves all quiver,
As the snail claims to be the fastest river.

The owl hoots jokes 'bout the mouse's dance,
While fireflies twirl in a soft romance.
The grass whispers secrets, soon to be heard,
All while the willow spreads the word.

In laughter, the night grows playful and bright,
Nature's hall of fame, what a delightful sight!
With every giggle, the stars join the play,
In the arms of the willow, all worries decay.

Whispers of Petal Dreams

A rose in bloom begins to hum,
It thinks it's got a great big drum.
The daisies giggle, they can't control,
As petals sway and spin, oh how they roll!

The marigolds dress in vibrant hues,
Arguing loudly 'bout the best of views.
Butterflies flutter, their laughter a swirl,
In a dance that makes the flowers all twirl.

A dandelion dressed in fluffy white,
Claims to hold secrets of the night.
With every puff, dreams scatter afar,
To a land of giggles, where jesters are stars.

As night falls softly, the flowers gleam,
Crafting stories more wild than a dream.
In whispers of petals, each tale is a jest,
Nature's own humor, forever the best!

The Enchanted Garden's Tale

In an enchanted garden where laughter lives,
Trees wear hats made of squirrel's fibs.
The roses throw petals like confetti in flight,
While the bees buzz loudly, 'What a fright, what a fright!'

The gnomes in a corner argue and bicker,
Over their favorite, the garden's biggest sticker.
Each mushroom grins wide, holding its ground,
As the laughter echoes, a magical sound.

A hedgehog sings of a prickly affair,
While the butterflies giggle, flapping in air.
The sun winks at everyone, casting a glow,
With a wink and a nudge, they all steal the show.

And as day turns to dusk, the fun won't cease,
In an enchanted garden, where joys never freeze!
With each little creature, a story to weave,
The humor of nature, you won't want to leave!

The Secret Life of Dewdrops

Dewdrops dance on leaves at dawn,
Twinkling like elves from dreams they've drawn.
They giggle and sway in the morning light,
But vanish too quick, oh what a sight!

They hide from the sun's relentless cheer,
Whispering secrets only they can hear.
Rolling down petals, they slide with glee,
A slippery game of hide and seek spree!

Plump little orbs in a jolly parade,
With each gentle breeze, their plans are delayed.
Mischief they sow, with shimmer and glow,
Then giggle away, like sneaky little pros!

At dusk they retreat, giggling still,
Dreaming of mischief, oh what a thrill.
But the flowers await, their tales to share,
Of dewdrop adventures floating in air!

Rhapsody of Roots and Reveries

Roots deep below throw a funky feast,
Sipping on soil like fine wine at least.
With whispers of earth and fun gregarious,
They plot the next trick, oh so nefarious!

They mingle with critters, a raucous crowd,
Tickling toes of the trees, feeling proud.
A tap dancing party beneath the ground,
Where foot-stomping fungi spin round and round!

"Let's plant some jokes in the garden tonight,"
Roots shout in laughter, their eyes shining bright.
They twist and twirl, with a hearty cheer,
Creating a rhapsody all can hear!

As stars blink above in the velvet sky,
Roots chuckle and sway, oh my, oh my!
Life's a soft whisper from leaf tops above,
While roots spin tales, bubbling over with love!

The Legend of the Lost Lavender

Once grew a lavender, bright and bold,
Whose fragrance was more than legends told.
It wandered away with a giggle and swish,
To find a new home, its one wily wish!

Through dales and valleys, it traveled with flair,
Dancing with breezes, it floated in air.
The bees looked perplexed, where did it go?
"Missing our queen, blooming deep in the snow?"

A quest was launched, with petals in plight,
Searching for lavender in moonlit night.
But it found a new joke, a nickname so sly,
"Lavender Lost, but oh my, oh my!"

The garden they found was a riotous place,
With daisies that giggled and ran a mad race.
In the end, it stayed for a reason so clear,
Funny plants make the heart bloom with cheer!

The Tale of the Wandering Vine

There once was a vine, oh what a sight,
Stretching so wildly, it twirled with delight.
Climbing up fences, it made quite a fuss,
While neighbors peeked out, saying, "What's all this?"

"Oh, just a small climb, no worries at all!"
It chuckled and wiggled, feeling so tall.
With each lofty leap, it tickled a wall,
Causing the garden to burst into call!

"Hey there, sweet flowers, do you see what I see?
A world all around, wild and free to be!"
A sunbeam, a giggle, a playful breeze,
The vine wrapped around, doing just as it please!

The garden was buzzing, with laughter aglow,
As the vine told tales of places to go.
So if you see it on any fine day,
Join in the fun, and let life sway!

Whispers of the Wildwood

In the woods, the squirrels sing,
Telling tales of nuts and spring.
A fox in shoes that didn't fit,
Chased a cat who loved to knit.

A rabbit with a funny hat,
Waltzed right by a sleepy cat.
With every hop, he'd boast and cheer,
"Who needs coffee? I've got my beer!"

Butterflies hold secret chats,
While juggling many little hats.
They jest and tease, oh what a sight,
In the dappled afternoon light.

So if you hear a giggle near,
Just follow it and have no fear.
For wildwood whispers on the breeze,
Are melodies of frolicsome trees.

The Secret Garden's Tale

A garden gnome, so round and stout,
He guards the flowers, there's no doubt.
With every muffle, chuckle, and grin,
He dreams of winning a dance-off win.

The daisies dance in silly rows,
While tulips play their toes in prose.
A sunflower with a funny grin,
Saves the day with a spin and spin.

Mice holding a grand debate,
On who can dance, oh isn't it great?
The hedgehogs hum a merry tune,
As fireflies start to light the moon.

So garden's secrets hide in jest,
Transforming weaves of joy and rest.
A place where laughter blooms and grows,
In every petal, mischief flows.

Petals in the Moonlight

Under moonlight, petals wink,
They're giggling, what do you think?
A flower whispered to a bee,
"Let's throw a ball, just you and me!"

The daisies donned their fancy clothes,
While tulips made up silly prose.
A dashing rose, with thorny shoes,
Joined the dance to win or lose.

Crickets served as DJs too,
Spinning tales of honeydew.
They jumped and twirled in pure delight,
As petals bounced through the night.

If you glimpse this jolly show,
Be sure to bring some seeds to throw.
For laughter blooms in forms so bright,
With petals dancing in the night.

The Enchanted Meadow

In the meadow, shadows play,
A bumblebee who loves ballet.
A sheep in socks, twirled left and right,
Complaining that the grass isn't right.

The daisies giggled, 'Oh dear me!
Can you believe the sight we see?'
A ladybug in a tiny car,
Drove past a snail, 'Don't drive so far!'

A rabbit wore a cape of thyme,
Proclaiming he was king sublime.
But what he didn't know for sure,
Is that he tripped on daisies pure.

So if you wander by this place,
You'll surely catch a silly face.
For in the meadow, humor swells,
In every laugh, it surely dwells.

The Wayward Willow's Wisdom

A willow hung low, thought she was a tree,
She danced in the wind, just a bit too free.
"Oh no!" cried the oak, "You're a sight to see!"
"Stop bending so far, you're not a bumblebee!"

In the midst of the park, she twirled like a shade,
While squirrels took bets on how she'd degrade.
"My branches don't care, I'm a cool leafy maid!"
She giggled and swayed, a nature charade!

With a flick of her leaves, she started a trend,
Other trees joined in, on branches they'd bend.
"Let's have a dance off, bring your forest friends!"
And thus, with a chuckle, the party transcends.

So next time you're lost in a woodland wide,
Look for the willow, with leaves open wide.
Join in her frolic, take joy in the ride,
For nature's got wisdom, if you laugh beside!

Fables of the Fern and Fernal Forest

In a glen full of ferns, a wise one did dwell,
She told tiny tales, with a giggle and swell.
"What's green and can't sing? A sprout in its shell!"
Where stories unfold, and riddles compel!

The ferns all agreed, a party we'll throw,
With laughter and whispers, they started to go.
They danced in the moonlight, with a splendorous glow,
Each swish of a leaf, set the night in a flow!

A snail brought a hat, a beetle some cheese,
They feasted till dawn, with incredible ease.
"What's slimy and bright? Just a joke with some breeze!"
And laughter erupted, floating high like the trees!

So next time you wander, through ferns lush and dense,
Remember the tales, laughter's just a few pence.
With friends who are silly, fun will commence,
In the depths of the green, joy's always immense!

A Rose's Riddle in the Rain

A rose in the garden wore droplets of dew,
She chuckled aloud, "What am I to do?"
"A riddle for bees, and a puzzle for you!"
"If you're just a red flower, what's really your hue?"

The daisies just laughed, petals bobbing with cheer,
"Oh Rose, you're the star, so we all persevere!"
"What's thorny yet sweet? Be honest my dear!"
She blushed with a grin, "I'm not being sincere!"

The rain tapped a beat, on her delicate leaves,
All flowers conspired, can't help but believe!
"What's fragrant and bright, but can also deceive?"
They pondered and pondered, while giggling with ease!

So when you're out walking, and gardens abound,
Keep eyes peeled for roses, careful, not drowned!
For laughter blooms brightly where riddles are found,
In each petal's secret, new joys will surround!

Tales from the Thicket

In the heart of the thicket, wild critters convened,
With foxes and rabbits, a mischiefful scene.
A hedgehog recounted a story so keen,
"What's prickly and nice? A joke unforeseen!"

They gathered around, for a night filled with fun,
Singing silly songs, till the early morn sun.
"What hops and can't talk? Now that's a good pun!"
With chatter and giggles, the evening was won!

A badger chimed in, holding berries so bright,
"These treats are the best! Have a bite, take a bite!"
What's furry and sweet, hidden just out of sight?
"Why, it's berry flavored mishaps, if eaten at night!"

So if you should stumble on a thicket of cheer,
Join in with the creatures, feel laughter draw near.
For in every tall tale, it's joy you will steer,
In the company of critters, each giggle sincere!

Where Shadows Dance with Light

In a garden where giggles grow,
The daisies ask, 'What about the snow?'
With sunbeams tickling the leafy green,
The bugs breakdance, it's quite the scene.

A squirrel wearing socks snug and bright,
Tells all his friends, 'I'm quite the sight!'
The shadows sway, and chuckles start,
As petals plot a secret art.

The daisies debate about fashion flair,
While butterflies gossip in the air.
A chubby bee with a curious grin,
Wonders how wild roses can spin.

In this garden, where laughter explodes,
Every flower knows its playful codes.
They play tag in the sun's warm embrace,
A jolly jubilee, a frolicsome place.

The Blossom's Dream

Once a bud had a whimsical wish,
To dance like a fish in a literary dish.
With petals outstretched in a twinkling breeze,
She pranced in the light, just aiming to please.

The wind was a jester, making her sway,
As ants held a meeting, deciding the way.
They debated her talent, all in a huddle,
While clovers just cackled and broke into muddle.

A ladybug joined with a pipe in her mouth,
Singing ballads of love from the North to the South.
The blossoms all giggled, their laughter a stream,
For flowers, they knew, lived within a dream.

So every night, when the moon took a peek,
The petals uncurled, and they'd dance till the week.
With the stars as their audience, they spun and twirled,
In the blossom's sweet dream, a whole new world.

Legends in the Lilac

In the shadow of lilacs, legends are spun,
Of gnomes in leisure, just having their fun.
With hats made of thyme and boots of soft moss,
They juggle ripe berries, but what a toss!

One gnome took a tumble, quite comical sight,
His buddies all laughed, 'You can't fly, hold tight!'
The lilacs just chuckled, swaying in glee,
As the sun made a joke, 'Don't you dare flee!'

A butterfly swooped in, a performer elite,
Stirring the lilac while tapping his feet.
'Who needs a stage when you have a warm breeze,
And a gnome's funny fall, amidst the tall trees?'

So the lilacs all whispered of joy in the air,
As gnomes danced around without a single care.
And if you think them silly, just wait 'til you see,
For laughter's the flower, in the heart of the tree.

The Gossamer Path

Down by the brook, where the ferns like to gossip,
Lived a snail named Sid, with a shell quite a posh whip.
He claimed he could run, oh what a surprise,
While ladybugs chuckled with sparkles in their eyes.

Sid slid on the stones, just as slick as can be,
Challenging beetles, as brave as you see.
They lined on the path, ready to cheer,
With petals applauding and tickles of cheer.

A dragonfly flew by, winking her eye,
She whispered to Sid, 'You think you can fly?'
But he just giggled, his shell shining bright,
Bouncing down blooms, what a marvelous sight!

So if you stroll down the gossamer way,
You might meet Sid, who'll make your day play.
With laughter and dreams in the air that you breathe,
The funny little snail believes he can weave.

Whimsical Whispers of Willow Wisps

In a grove of green, the breeze did play,
Twisting twigs in a jig, all day.
The bushes chuckle, the branches dance,
As squirrels in suits try their luck with romance.

A rabbit in top hat hops with flair,
While dampened daisies curl, unaware.
They gossip of bees who wear tiny shoes,
While butterflies mimic the latest news.

The sunbeams giggle, the shadows sway,
Painting portraits of mischief in the hay.
With whispers of whimsy, the willy-nillys,
Make each blunder a tale of silly lilies.

The Ballad of Gossamer Gypsy Vines

Oh, gossamer vines, entwined and spry,
Climbing up fences, as fast as you fly.
With ambitions of grandeur and leafy dreams,
They host tiny parties with firefly beams.

A jaunty old snail with a hat made of bark,
Tells tall tales to frogs that croak in the dark.
They roll in the clover and dash through the dew,
Proclaiming the flowers are all wearing blue!

In the midst of the laughter, a gust rolls through,
Tickling the blooms, as if on cue.
The vines start to waltz with the daisies,
While dandelions prance like old-time crazies.

Fantasies Among Fungi

Beneath the great oaks, where mushrooms bloom,
A party erupts in the forest's womb.
Toadstools in tuxes spin under the moon,
While fairies make music with spoons and a tune.

A wise old truffle with glasses and cane,
Tells jokes of the rain that fell like champagne.
Slugs in their shorts slide sideways with ease,
As the playful rainworms do jazzy trapeze.

In the soft, mossy carpet, the night unfolds,
As crickets share secrets that the night holds.
Join the dance of the spores as they drift,
For the laughter of fungi is truly a gift.

Mariners of Meadow's Marina

In a meadow where lilies pretend to be boats,
The minnows sing songs, with merry little notes.
Ladybugs sail with intricate maps,
While snails in the breezes take curious laps.

Cattails like masts hoist flags made of fluff,
While dragonflies dart, saying, 'Isn't this stuff?
The bees are the crew, buzzing tales of the dew,
Declaring, 'We've found some sweet nectar for two!'

With teacups of petals, they gather for tea,
Sharing wild tales of the swirling sea.
Under the sky that glimmers and glows,
The mariners laugh as the merriment flows.

Timeless Blooms of Serendipity

In the garden of giggles, they sway,
Sunflowers winking at the bee's ballet.
Dancing dandelions toss their hair,
While daisies whisper, "Do we dare?"

A thistle told tales of a knight,
Who tripped on his armor in broad daylight.
With petals for shields and roots for swords,
They fought off boredom with laughter in hordes.

The tulips wore hats, oh what a sight,
Holding court with the moon every night.
They quipped and they joked, with petals aflame,
While the violets nodded, joining the game.

Through the blooms, the chuckles unfurl,
A riot of color, a comical swirl.
In nature's embrace, with joy so free,
It's the silliest patch in the world, you see!

The Sylvan Storyteller

In the woods where whispers abound,
A squirrel spins tales from the ground.
With acorns for actors, they humor the breeze,
While the laughter of leaves joins in with ease.

A raccoon wearing spectacles, sharp and bright,
Reads from a book by the soft moonlight.
The chapters are wild, the words a surprise,
As mushrooms nod knowingly, oh how they rise!

The owls hoot jokes to the frogs at the brook,
While fireflies buzz with a sweet, mellow look.
A dance of the critters, a light-hearted raid,
In a forest where stories are never delayed.

With each giggle shared in the night,
The stars twinkle down, feeling quite right.
The storyteller bows, the crowd gives a cheer,
In the book of the woods, there's no room for fear!

In the Heart of the Thicket

In a thicket so thick, where the laughter blooms,
Foxes perform plays in their fancy costumes.
With a tap of their tails and a flick of their ears,
They dance 'round the bushes, forgetting their fears.

A snail tells a tale, all slow and grand,
As critters gather round, all close at hand.
With a twist of the shell and a wink of his eye,
They roll in the dew, 'til the dawn's sky runs dry.

The hedgehogs hum sonnets, all prickly and sweet,
While rabbits play drums with their rhythmic feet.
A raucous affair under branches and leaves,
In the heart of the thick, where humor believes.

Amidst this commotion, the flowers laugh bright,
Tickled by petals that dance with delight.
In this quirky thicket, where silliness thrives,
The joy of the wild in each chuckle survives!

The Rose's Requiem

In a garden bloomed a rose, quite the champ,
Deciding one day to host a grand rampe.
With petals as seats, and thorns for the zest,
Invitations were sent to nature's best guest.

The daisies brought snacks that were nothing but green,
While sunflowers laughed at the cooking routine.
The violets giggled, all caught in a sneeze,
As the wind blew with humor, bringing leaves to their knees.

A bumblebee buzzed in, making a fuss,
Claiming his honey was better than us.
But a ladybug tossed him a witty remark,
"Your dance is a buzzkill, but we're still in the park!"

At the end of the night, with jokes in full bloom,
The rose, oh so regal, announced from her room:
"Let's lift a petal to laughter and cheer,
For every sweet moment that brings us all near!"

Echoes of the Forest Floor

In the depths where the mushrooms grow,
A squirrel donned a hat that stole the show.
He danced with the ants, quite a sight to behold,
Chasing shadows of stories, both silly and bold.

The leaves whispered secrets of mischief and cheer,
As rabbits recounted their antics with beer.
They tripped over roots in a giggling spree,
While owls hooted softly, 'What folly, oh me!'

A hedgehog rolled by in a flashy red car,
Singing to crickets, 'You ain't seen my scar!'
With a wink and a wink, he dashed on his way,
Leaving laughter behind, like confetti of play.

So listen, dear friend, to the forest's own tune,
Where giggles and wiggles come under the moon.
For in every corner, a jest waits to bloom,
In the echoing laughter of nature's grand room.

Beneath the Canopy's Embrace

Under branches where mischief unfolds,
Caterpillars tell tales that tickle the molds.
They whisper of kings with crowns made from grass,
While the bees share the gossip of flowers that pass.

The foxes play tricks with a wink and a grin,
Spilling the tea, oh what chaos begins!
With a snap of a twig, the laughter erupts,
As the whole forest watches their plans go corrupt.

A raccoon in goggles, surveying his loot,
Disguised as a chef in a fanciful suit.
'What's for dinner?' he asked, with a twist of his tail,
'Why, the finest of berries, from the wild to the trail!'

So dance under leaves, let your worries take flight,
For beneath this green blanket, all troubles feel light.
With chuckles abounding, let joy lead the race,
In this whimsical world, beneath nature's embrace.

The Tale of the Wandering Vine

A vine claimed its fame with a curious crawl,
It twisted and turned, causing quite the sprawl.
With a joie de vivre, it danced through the air,
Tickling old trunks with a cheeky, bold flair.

It tangled with flowers in a playful chase,
Whispering jokes that made petals embrace.
'Why wear proper shoes when you can just flow?'
And the blooms laughed aloud, waving to and fro.

But one day, a gopher with a penchant for doom,
Said, 'My dear vine, beware of the broom!'
Yet the vine just giggled, 'A sweep of my dreams,
I'll twirl around trouble, or so it seems!'

So tangled and happy, it danced without care,
Spreading the joy of its whimsical flair.
For in every twist, there's a tale to divine,
Of a vine that just wanted to wander and shine.

Secrets of the Garden Nymph

In a garden where gnomes have a laugh and a joke,
Lives a nymph who delights in the things that she spoke.
'What's better than daisies?' she giggled with glee,
'A cabbage that winks when it sees me!'

With petals for skirts and a crown of fine thyme,
She orchestrates parties, all dressed up in rhyme.
With a wink to the sun and a nod to the moon,
She leads the shy violets to dance to her tune.

Then came a mistake, a frog was in disguise,
Hopping to show that he also could rise.
But tripping on roots, he fell with a splash,
And the nymph just roared with a merry belly laugh.

So heed the wise words of a garden so fair,
Where laughter, not worry, is the magic we share.
For in every leaf lie secrets divine,
That life can be funny, just like this nymph's rhyme.

Legends of the Forest's Heart

In the woods, where squirrels dance,
A rabbit wore a silly pants.
They laughed until the sun set low,
Tales of acorns in a row.

A wise old owl gave a wink,
Said, "Don't eat nuts, just have a drink!"
But the raccoon favored pies,
Underneath the starry skies.

The fox told tales of shoes so bright,
He tripped and fell—oh, what a sight!
While badger snored in comfy muck,
Dreaming of his favorite luck.

A deer adorned with flower crowns,
Pranced around, ignoring frowns.
Every creature joined the fun,
In this heart where laughter's spun.

The Orchid's Midnight Secret

In the garden, shadows creep,
An orchid whispers while we sleep.
With petals soft and secrets deep,
It tells of dreams that make us leap.

A gnome with mischief in his eyes,
Planted shoes beneath the skies.
He thought they'd grow in fiery red,
But instead, a dragon said, "Let's spread!"

A raccoon tried to sneak a peek,
At blooms that giggled, so to speak.
But tripped on roots, and oh, what brash—
He tumbled in with a big splat crash.

The moonlit kisses glow and twine,
Each flower laughs, it's all divine.
So join the dance, give it a whirl,
In this night where petals swirl.

A Symphony of Scented Shadows

In the dusk, the jasmine sways,
As fireflies hum their gentle praise.
A beetle's band strikes up a tune,
While mushrooms gather 'neath the moon.

The lavender teased with fragrant sighs,
And daisies winked with tiny eyes.
A painted lady in her dress,
Said, "Scented shadows bring such zest!"

The garden snickered, soft and bright,
As corncob popped with all its might.
A chorus of giggles filled the air,
From every blossom without a care.

So let's all dance and spin about,
In this scented spree, there's no doubt.
With every bloom, a note to share,
In the symphony of scents so rare.

Echoes in the Lilac Breeze

In lilac fields, the stories twirl,
A windy tale of a cheeky girl.
She tied her hair to petals bright,
And laughed with bees till late at night.

A butterfly grinned, sipping tea,
While telling tales of flying free.
With every flap, the stories soared,
Of plants that giggled, never bored.

A clumsy hedgehog found a hat,
He couldn't walk, fell with a splat!
The daisies burst in laughter grand,
As he rolled over on the land.

So join the fun, let laughter tease,
In every rustle of the breeze.
The lilacs giggle, shout with ease,
In echoes sweet, may joy increase.

Sagas Beneath the Skyscraping Trees

Beneath the trees so tall and green,
A squirrel hoards all that he's seen.
With acorns stacked like tiny towers,
   He dreams of nutty, nutty hours.

A bird with a flair sings songs so bold,
While gossiping leaves share tales of old.
   The rabbits dress in cotton attire,
And dance on the grass around a fire.

A ladybug boasts with a polka dot shine,
While ants form a line, claiming it's fine.
'Who's in charge?' a beetle does bray,
   The laughter erupts in leafy ballet.

Under the shadows where shadows retreat,
   The mischief unfolds on four tiny feet.
   Each day a new saga begins to tease,
In the chaos of chuckles beneath the trees.

The Chronicles of the Quaking Aspen

In the grove of gold with leaves that shake,
A group of trees makes merriment break.
With whispers of wind and a rustle of cheer,
They plot silly tricks when no one is near.

A chipmunk in stripes thinks he's a great boss,
While dizzy little owls just roll in the moss.
'Let's swap our branches!' the youngest one cries,
So they weave and they bobble, creating new ties.

Fashioned in bark, they sport new designs,
With bark beards and mustaches, they look so divine.
A gust of wind sends them all in a twirl,
And laughter erupts with a skip and a whirl.

The moonlight spills gossip upon all the boughs,
Like a party in forest, with nary a pause.
Underneath the stars, they shake and they prance,
In the Chronicles of joy, every tree's a romance.

Caspia's Coral Canopy

In a forest where colors like sunsets collide,
Caspia's canopy spreads out wide.
With blooms in pinks and hues that shine,
Toft creatures giggle and swap tales divine.

A butterfly wearing a glittering suit,
Invites all the flowers to dance with a hoot.
While bees buzz along with a rhythm so bold,
They craft sticky stories that never grow old.

A hedgehog dons petals, a real floral star,
While frogs serenade from the side of the spar.
Each leaf holds a secret with laughter entwined,
Making fun of the fables that grew in their minds.

In Caspia's dream of the whimsical hues,
Every critter knows how to lighten the blues.
So join if you venture where wonders grow free,
In the dance of the silly, you're sure to agree!

The Enchanted Ecosystem

In ecosystems where humor is grand,
Trees tell stories that are quite unplanned.
The dandelions laugh, spreading seeds in delight,
While mushrooms join in for a wild night.

A hedgehog with humor tries stand-up on stage,
While a wise old toad gives advice of the age.
'Don't eat that fly!' he croaks with a grin,
'It's your turn to hop in this whimsical spin!'

A porcupine juggles with prickles in hand,
To rumbles of laughter that echo the land.
Bugs barter secrets and giggle anew,
In the dance of the leaves, the fun never skews.

So wander the paths where the merriment flows,
'Round trees with tales and jokes that each knows.
In this enchanted display of zest and of cheer,
The ecosystem thrives, year after year.

Secrets Beneath the Bark

In the wood, a tale unfolds,
A squirrel's secret, never told.
With acorns stacked, a treasure chart,
He laughs alone, a woodland art.

The owls roll eyes, they think him mad,
His plans for winter, oh so bad!
But when the snowflakes start to fall,
He's sipping cocoa, not bothered at all.

Underneath, the roots all giggle,
As Mr. Squirrel starts to wiggle.
A dance of joy, atop his stash,
A nutty party, quite a bash!

So if you wander through the trees,
Remember laughter rides the breeze.
For nature's lore is full of cheer,
In every bark, a joke is near.

Chronicles of the Wild Blossom

In the meadow where daisies bloom,
A daft young bee was full of zoom.
He chased a flower, oh so bright,
And bumped his nose, what a sight!

The petals giggled, green grass swayed,
As buzzing tales of clumsiness played.
Each blunder shared with a sunny grin,
A comic twist to the flower's spin.

But when the day grew tired and slow,
The bee found solace in the glow.
With all his pals, they'd share their dreams,
Of pollen parties and honeyed schemes.

Through every buzz and every laugh,
The flowers write their quirky graph.
A world of wonders, bright and loud,
Where giggles bloom beneath the cloud.

The Language of Leaves

Leaves whisper secrets, so it seems,
Each rustle holds a world of dreams.
A crinkled leaf wearing a frown,
Swears it was once the talk of the town.

A sprightly bud beams in the sun,
Claiming it's now the number one!
"Last year's gossip, look at me grow!"
While the autumns just chuckle below.

The wind plays tricks, swirling their tales,
As old branches share ancient gales.
From funny to wise, the leaves all chime,
Telling their stories, one leaf at a time.

So if you sit beneath their shade,
Listen closely, don't be delayed.
For laughter rustles in the breeze,
In the language of leaves, oh such tease!

Stories Woven in Thorns

In a prickly bush, a tale unfolds,
Where brave little bugs dared to be bold.
One said, "I'll climb, I'll reach for the stars,"
But he got stuck, the thorns gave scars!

A ladybug giggled, "Oh dear friend!
You should've stuck to the grass, not ascend!"
But amidst the ouch, a wisdom grew,
That even sharp paths can lead to new.

The thorns told jokes, with a twist of fate,
While the brave bug blushed, feeling quite great.
A thorny crown, a regal sight,
He got his laugh, despite the fright.

So if you wander where brambles lie,
Remember laughter waves bye-bye.
For stories woven in the spines,
Bring playful twists with nature's signs.

Harmony in the Hydrangea's Harbor

In a garden where giggles grow,
Hydrangeas sway to the breeze's flow.
Bees wear sunglasses for their flight,
And butterflies dance under the moonlight.

A snail in a top hat slides with grace,
While ants throw a wild, wiggly race.
They cheer for the tulips, red and tall,
Except for a daffodil, who trips and falls.

The grasshoppers sing a tune so bright,
To mushrooms that twirl, what a sight!
While worms hold a conga line,
And all of nature feels quite fine.

So come join the fun in the vibrant land,
Where every bloom has a joke so grand.
Laughter echoes through leafy halls,
In the harbor where merriment calls.

The Myth of the Melodious Moss

Once upon a mossy mound,
Lived a chorus that had no sound.
The rocks rolled their eyes in disbelief,
As mushrooms plotted a musical chief.

A frog leapt in with a shiny crown,
Declared himself king of the slimy town.
He croaked a tune that made plants sway,
While crickets jumped in a cabaret.

The sneaky squirrels brought treats galore,
Popcorn and acorns, who could want more?
But squirrels danced wildly, nibbled too fast,
And one tripped, sending a snack storm to blast!

The tale has spread through the leaf and vine,
Of moss that sings if you treat it fine.
So if your garden needs some cheer,
Invite the moss; it will appear!

The Parable of the Perseverant Pansy

A pansy perched on the garden wall,
Claimed she could outshine them all.
With petals so bright and a bold little stance,
She started each day with a flamboyant dance.

The daisies giggled, the roses just sighed,
But pansy, undeterred, had blooming pride.
She painted her face with droplets of dew,
And challenged the bees to a duel or two.

With each whirling gust and each brave little sway,
Pansy held strong, come what may.
The sun even winked at her vibrant display,
While rabbits stopped dancing and decided to stay.

In the end, she showed all her resilient flair,
In a patch of the garden that echoed her dare.
So next time you see a bold little bloom,
Remember her courage in the green room.

Dances in Dew-Kissed Darkness

At midnight when the moon starts to glow,
The flowers hold a party, a secret show.
With petals a-twinkle, they leap and prance,
In bubbles of laughter, they whirl and dance.

The nightingale chirps a melodious tune,
While fireflies flash in a fervent swoon.
The daisies twist and spin with glee,
While the thistle gleefully spills its tea.

Gnomes tap their toes in the grass so fine,
As mushrooms take turns, they waltz in a line.
With giggles and wiggles, the shadows ignite,
While roses blush pinker under starlit night.

So tiptoe to this garden so rare,
Join in the fun without any care.
For every bloom shines, with laughter and cheer,
In the dances of darkness, all are welcome here.

Mavericks of the Meadow

In a field where daisies dance,
Came a rabbit with a rather strange prance.
He wore a hat that was far too tall,
Claiming he could leap over any wall.

A beetle laughed, then tried to fly,
But spun in circles, oh my oh my!
With a wink and a skip, they joined a race,
That ended with a pie in each one's face!

The butterflies cheered, they fluttered and sighed,
As the friends grew tired and decided to glide.
With laughter that echoed through the sunny glen,
They plotted for mischief, again and again!

So beware the meadow, where fun multiplies,
With odd little critters and curious lies.
For when the sun sets and the moon is bright,
The mavericks gather, ready for flight!

The Curious Case of the Collapsing Canopy

Underneath the trees, a mystery stirs,
Why do the squirrels wear fuzzy old furs?
They claim it's for style, or maybe a scheme,
To hide from the crows and pursue their dream.

One day they gathered, a council of sorts,
To decide if the furs were enough for the ports.
A wise old owl, with glasses askew,
Suggested a wig; perhaps, even two!

With giggles and glee, they dressed up in style,
A fashion parade that stretched for a mile.
They pranced through the forest, laughing out loud,
Till the trees started shaking and bows bent so proud.

But the canopy trembled, then gave such a clatter,
As the squirrels got stuck, caught in each other's chatter.
So now they just wear their own fluffy coats,
And leave the fine fashion to floating old boats!

Anemone's Allure Unveiled

In a garden where giggles bloom right and left,
Lived Anemone, charming, but slightly inept.
She tried to impress on a bright summer day,
Yet tripped on her petals, and fell in dismay.

The bees buzzed around with a curious hum,
As Anemone cried, "I'm not such a bum!"
With a wiggle, she danced, and forgot her despair,
Only for snails to declare, "Why go anywhere?"

So they joined in her folly, the garden struck gold,
As the laughter erupted, a sight to behold.
With butterflies twirling, and sunbeams that shined,
They celebrated blunders, and love entwined.

Now Anemone shines with her friends all around,
For fun can be found just by falling on ground.
With humor and heart, she leads the parade,
In the garden of laughter, where no one's afraid!

Sonnet of the Saffron Solstice

As saffron sunsets paint the sky bright,
The flowers hold gatherings, oh what a sight!
The daisies debate on who bakes the best pie,
While the sunflowers giggle, oh me, oh my!

The bees in their buzz suggest a cook-off,
Said a rose with a grin, "I'll show you who's boss!"
But violets chimed in with a sweet little tune,
"Let's dance 'round this table until we're to swoon!"

And the garden erupted in petals and glee,
With thyme in their step and fresh mint for the tea.
As shadows grew long on that solstice eve,
They vowed to make laughter the life they believe.

So here's to the blooms who find joy in the day,
In the dance of the sun, they'll forever stay.
With humor and jest in the saffron glow,
Life's sweetest of fables, forever will grow!

The Lark's Song Among the Petunias

A lark perched high, with a jestful flair,
Sings to the blooms with a style most rare.
Petunias giggle, their colors bright,
As bees do a tango, what a sight!

A dancing flower with a cheeky grin,
Wags its petals, invites the wind in.
With each little flutter, they cause a scene,
In a vibrant world, oh so serene.

Butterflies chuckle, their wings all a-flutter,
Making their rounds through the floral clutter.
Larks laugh back with a melodious cheer,
In this riot of color, there's naught to fear.

Under the sun in a whimsical play,
Nature's own jesters come out to sway.
With laughter and song, they brighten the day,
In this garden of joy, forever they'll stay.

Threads of the Fabled Orchid

An orchid spun tales, oh what a weave,
Of mischief and giggles, who'd dare not believe?
With petals of magic, it twisted the night,
Its colors igniting the stars, what a sight!

Worms whispered secrets, they're crafty and sly,
In a dance with the roots, they spun and they'd fly.
A dragonfly giggled, quite bold and spry,
As it zipped all around with a flippity cry.

The moon peeked in, with a chuckle so bright,
As blossoms told tales of their playful delight.
With every soft rustle, the garden conspired,
In threads of bright laughter, they never got tired.

So next time you wander where petals compose,
Remember the stories that bloom like a rose.
For in every garden, life has its own jest,
A tale woven sweetly, always expressed.

The Call of the Wild Chrysanthemum

A wild mum called out with a raspy cheer,
"To scatter some giggles, come one, come near!"
With petals like laughter, it spread the fun,
As daisies rejoiced beneath the bright sun.

The gales joined in, with a breezy laugh,
Pushing the blossoms down a silly path.
Bees buzzing around, with their sweet little hums,
Joined in the banter, oh what a sum!

A tumbleweed giggled, dancing along,
In this bright patch of petals, nothing was wrong.
Each bloom had a jest, a delightful play,
As the wild mum led them, brightening the day.

So if you should hear from the fields up ahead,
A rumble of laughter beneath the sun spread,
Know that the flowers are having a ball,
In the garden of cheer, there's a party for all!

A Journey Through Gnarled Roots

Upon gnarled roots, a story unfolds,
Of critters and laughter, a treasure to behold.
Worms with sunglasses and snails on a spree,
Sliding down branches, oh what glee!

A squirrel in jest, with a nut as his prop,
Jumps 'round with vigor, then does a flip flop.
The mushrooms are chuckling, all in their caps,
As the stories cascade in uproarious flaps.

Through tangled old roots, where giggles reside,
A rabbit in slippers takes a joyous stride.
With friends on the journey, all fur and delight,
In the heart of the woods, they dance through the night.

So join in the laughter, in nature's own nook,
Where the gnarled roots whisper, in every good book.
For in this whimsical world, life's always in tune,
With funny little critters, beneath the bright moon.

Kaleidoscope of the Kangaroo Paw

In a garden where the colors play,
Kangaroo paws dance in the sun's ray.
They wiggle and jiggle with such delight,
Creating a show that feels just right.

A cat in a hat joins the ruckus too,
Sipping on nectar, oh what a view!
The flowers giggle, the leaves all cheer,
As butterflies whisper, 'Let's stay right here!'

A wallaby strums on a tiny lute,
While roos in sunglasses clap to the flute.
It's a floral fiesta, come one, come all,
Where the colors of laughter brightly enthrall.

So if ever you wander where odd things bloom,
Remember the paws that dance in a room.
For in this wild garden of cheer so spry,
You'd laugh till you cry as the flowers fly.

Reveries of the Running Rose

A rose sprouted legs, ready to dash,
With petals like sneakers, what a flash!
It raced through the garden, oh what a sight,
While bees buzzed around in sheer delight.

A tulip held signs, 'Race you to spring!'
And daisies cheered loud—oh, what joy they bring!
With each little twist, the roses would spin,
Singing silly songs, embracing the win.

But vines tangled up in a knotty mess,
Saying, 'Don't rush, darling, life's more or less!'
They laughed and they played, decided to stroll,
For running's just funny if it's good for the soul.

So wander the paths where roses could run,
Where laughter's the prize and humor's the fun.
In a world that's all petals, you might just find,
That a sprightly old rose can leave sorrows behind.

The Siren Song of the Sunflower

In a field of sunflowers swaying so bold,
One sang sweetly, its voice pure gold.
It wooed the bees with a catchy refrain,
While butterflies twirled in the soft summer rain.

A little ant danced on its golden face,
Saying, 'I swear, oh, you've got such grace!'
The petals all giggled, 'What a fine show!'
While the sunflower basked in its glorious glow.

But a wind came rushing with a mischievous tune,
Spinning sunflowers like a wild cartoon.
They twirled and they whirled, a hilarious sight,
As bugs fell off branches in pure delight.

So heed this sweet song, let it fill your heart,
For in laughter and joy, we all play a part.
Join the sunflowers and let your soul play,
In a world of bright petals, every day is a ballet!

Enigmas of the Ecstatic Evergreen

In a forest of evergreens, tall and wide,
The trees whisper secrets, they laugh, they guide.
One said, 'Why do squirrels wear little hats?'
The others just chuckled, 'To outsmart the cats!'

With branches that wiggle and needles that sway,
The trees held a party, come join the fray!
With pinecone confetti raining all around,
The smell of fresh laughter was lost and then found.

At twilight, they danced in the shimmering glow,
With shadows that whispered, 'Come on, let's go!'
One spry little sapling puffed out its chest,
'Who's the tallest here?' it jovially guessed.

But giggles erupted as the moonlight appeared,
And all of the trees felt so utterly cheered.
In the realm of the evergreens frolicking bold,
Each riddle unraveled as new tales unfold.

The Enigma of Eternal Eucalyptus

In the land of trees that dance and sway,
Eucalyptus played hide and seek all day.
With a wink and a nod, it tried to confound,
But only the koalas truly astound.

Those gum leaves shimmer, a prankster's delight,
Twisting tales in the soft moonlight.
"Why do we smell like a cough drop so bold?"
Asked a curious leaf, feeling quite old.

The answer was wrapped in a fragrant embrace,
A riddle that rolled in a witty old trace.
"Laugh with the wind, let your worries take flight,
For the secrets of trees are shared every night."

And so, as they giggled, the branches would creak,
Telling tales of their antics until the next week.
Eucalyptus, the jokester, so sprightly and bright,
Keeps the forest amused until dawn's early light.

Whispers of the Wildflower Wind

In fields where daisies dare to dream,
Whispers of wildflowers giggle and gleam.
They chat as they bloom, with secrets to share,
Each petal a story, floating in air.

A dandelion puff claimed a crown of fluff,
Said, "I'm the king, and yet, I'm not tough!"
With a puff of the breeze, he twirled with grace,
Sending wishes flying all over the place.

The violets cackled, they were up to some fun,
"Let's race with the tulips and see who can run!"
But roots got tangled, it turned into a mess,
Laughter erupted; it's chaos, no less.

So next time you wander through the blooms all around,
Listen closely to laughter; it's a magical sound.
For nature's own humor, like a bright sunny day,
Is woven in whispers that dance in the sway.

Ballads of the Bramble Patch

In a bramble patch where the berries grow,
Sang a hedgehog in a burly warm slow.
With spikes like a crown and a voice like a bell,
He spun wild ballads, casting a spell.

The blackberries buzzed with a sweet little tune,
While raspberries rolled, giggling under the moon.
"Let's throw a party!" cried a cheeky old vine,
"Bring your best flavor, let's make it divine!"

But thorns, feeling cheeky, decided to tease,
Stuck their noses in, and ate all the cheese.
Yet laughter erupted, they danced on the ground,
In a bramble-packed bash, where joy did abound.

So if you should wander and find such a mess,
Know that in life, it's the humor, no less.
The ballads of berries make merriment last,
In a world full of quirks, they've got a blast!

Chronicles of the Celestial Sedge

In the meadows where sedges sway and shout,
Lived a wise old owl with no fear of a drought.
He wore a small hat made of silky green threads,
Imparting his wisdom to all of the heads.

"Beneath the bright stars, let's ponder the day,
And ponder the odd ways we all like to play.
The frogs croak their pranks from the murky old bog,
While fireflies hover, like a light-up smog!"

Then came a raccoon, with mischief ablaze,
Wearing a mask that was flimsy and gaze.
"Well, what's our next scheme, oh wise feathered plight?
Shall we dance on the banks till the morning is bright?"

And so they all chuckled, the critters aligned,
In chronicles woven by laughter entwined.
With sedge as their backdrop, they reveled in cheer,
Turning mishaps to fun, oh, how sweet to endear!

www.ingramcontent.com/pod-product-compliance
Lightning Source LLC
Chambersburg PA
CBHW071833160426
43209CB00003B/282